HARM

HARM

Alan Jenkins

Chatto & Windus
LONDON

First published in Great Britain in 1994

3 5 7 9 10 8 6 4 2

© Alan Jenkins 1994

Alan Jenkins has asserted his right under the
Copyright, Designs and Patents Act, 1988 to be
identified as the author of this work

Published in 1994 by
Chatto & Windus Limited
Random House, 20 Vauxhall Bridge Road
London SW1V 2SA

Random House Australia (Pty) Limited
20 Alfred Street, Milsons Point, Sydney
New South Wales 2061, Australia

Random House New Zealand Limited
18 Poland Road, Glenfield
Auckland 10, New Zealand

Random House South Africa (Pty) Limited
PO Box 337, Bergvlei, South Africa

Random House UK Limited Reg. No. 954009

A CIP catalogue record for this book is available from
the British Library

ISBN 0 7011 6106 X

Typeset by SX Composing Ltd, Rayleigh, Essex
Printed in Great Britain by
Mackays of Chatham PLC, Chatham, Kent

Grateful acknowledgement is made to the editors of
the following publications, in which some of these
poems first appeared: *New Statesman and Society*,
Pequod, Poetry Book Society Anthology 1992,
*The Times Literary Supplement, The Chatto Book
of the Devil.*

CONTENTS

For Nicola

I never kept a diary. I never saved up witty things people told me. I never even bothered to remember my own past, the events that mattered most to me. Nor have I tried to piece things together. I'm a master of the art of pruning, you might say, as though I'd heard that plants should be cut back to make them flourish – except I keep hacking them down to the roots and wonder why they die.

Now I forget everything, and for some time I have practised negligence and disorder. Yet you are everywhere beside me.

Edmund White, *Nocturnes for the King of Naples*

NOCTURNE

When young couples loving
beneath the unleaving
chestnut trees in Holland Park
fill me with loathing
of those who unclothing
lie wetly together in the dark,

when every good intended
like the harm unmended
is stripped and flayed by sodium light,
all that I've kept hidden
comes back unbidden,
and nothing, now, will be all right.

PRAGUE SPRING

I had been thinking all night of calling up
the Prague correspondent of *Libération*
for lunch, dinner, anything: grey-eyed, Parisienne,
skinny; we'd met the previous evening and though my cup
was running over, I wanted more, I wanted another ration
of her husky-voiced French-American accent . . .

I had been planning to suggest
that she and I track down a plate of something or other
in Prague's only game restaurant. She'd be my guest.
I'd been hoping she would look on me as a brother
in her mystery, despite my obvious lack
of dissident credentials, despite my sheen of luck

and privilege. Over drinks in the bar
at the Europa Hotel, I would recall how close I'd come
to a bomb-scare in the other Europa, in Belfast;
she would describe the friends she'd left at home,
her childhood places and the prison-memoir past
that had caught her and carried her this far . . .

Her voice, when I finally called,
was friendly, non-committal, but there was a note,
I thought, of impatience, boredom almost, as if to say,
*Don't you know there's been a revolution here? Can
   you not*
see yourself in ten years, fatter, richer, bald —
what else? Poems? Memories? Me one of them? No way.

VISITING

He visited, the man who takes your life
and turns it upside-down, from floor
to ceiling; and he saw I had no wife,
and saw the things that I had worked hard for
and smiled, as if he knew what went on *here*.

He visited the corner of my flat
where daily I had spooned out food
for my dainty-footed, air-sniffing cat
and through the summer, chunks left half-chewed
had poured rich smells into the atmosphere.

Flies visited the smells. They hung in heat
like helicopters seen from a distance,
they drooled and fed on rotting processed meat,
they laid their eggs. The buzzing small insistence
should have warned me, the cat not going near.

Friends visited, but no-one noticed anything.
And when he tore my carpet up, the man –
No lie, I nearly puked my ring.
I saw yellow-white seethe in a silver can
full of dank sawdust, a towpath by a weir –

I visited my father on the bank
where he and I went fishing each week-end;
the shrubs, the weir, the lock and river shrank,
our bicycles had vanished round a bend
and a high tide taken all our gear.

I visited my father in the pubs
where I had watched him drink away the hours
of talk or silence, piling up the stubs
in ashtrays, but the cigarettes were sour
and the bitter had an aftertaste of fear.

I visited my father by the sea
where he had scrubbed me with a gritty towel
and held me till I squirmed and struggled free;
I heard the gulls scream and the sea-wind howl,
the freezing water writhed and flung me clear.

I visited my father in his grave
and grubbed until I found all that was left –
a matchbook of maggots. *Grieve, grieve*
they whispered when I held it aloft,
Grieve, grieve when I put it to my ear.

ORKNEY

A hulk half-sunk in the mouth of Scapa Flo
brings back Sunday afternoons, my father, years ago,
Jack Hawkins starring, and the cat-and-mouse
played out between the echo-sounder and the sunken ones:
he sat transfixed, this desert rat, landlubber, Navy man
only in his dreams. And in his dreams for me –
who might by now have been fifteen years at sea,
Commander – *carrière ouverte aux talents* –
standing on the bridge, who instead have crossed by ferry
to hunch here, scribbling in a wind-strafed house
and drift on a tide of whisky to where the twelve-inch guns
lie sunk, and drift down, a pint, a quart, a gallon
to float up by the Tower Bridge Hotel, where you once
opened up to me, I drowned in you. Your Navy man.

SHIP OF FOOLS

How were they led to water, to chartering the leaky boat –
Old twin-berth, twelve knots, no mast or sail, no swivel
    chair:
Less than what you'd want, say, for a week-end's pottering
    around
In a tributary of the Teme, where you *could* run aground,
Drop anchor in a kiddies' paddling pool, or scare
A shoal of minnows, or capsize a boy's bobbing float –
Young men who in their daily lives oozed *savoir faire*,

Even under pressure, always knowing what was what?
Rescue them, can't we, from whatever brought them here,
South of everything they knew, to chance a fishing trip, a
Brothel and a salty bar, a boat without a skipper;
Opened them to influences of the tropics; showed them
    fear;
Amazed two stomachs shrivelled tightly to a single knot,
Then burst their lungs with blackness? No, it's written in
    the plot,

In the stars they could not read, in the pride their natures
    felt
Shrugging off the obstacles to things they chose to do,
Forcing all the world to grant their every slightest wish,
On the cutting edge of options, in the blind pursuit of fish;
United on this, that whatsoever they projected, few –
None, that's to say – objected to. No deal undealt,
Dirty trick untried, no shit unheaped on someone's dish . . .

*

They had drifted half a world from Cape Halfalump
While one of them tried to coax the fuel pump
Or untangle the screw, the rudder-thing, and the other sot
Made a meal of fish-heads and blood-smells and sat
Entranced by the click-click of his ratchet and his line
Nonchalantly winking in the sun. Then they were alone,
Massively, with the fish for company and something
    brewing

In the sky like a wet bruise, the slap of waves, the boat
    slewing
Sideways on to them, tiny, slung between two green-mauve
Spires of a sea-cathedral that was on the move.
Imagining the worst (and some imaginings are true),
Not knowing yet what it would be, they went below to try
Getting through with *Mayday* or an SOS – the radio-ham
    thing –
But neither of them knew how to work the damn thing.

Every hour that went by took them further from help;
Lower and lower came the sky, the sea rose like an Alp;
In no time, their few supplies were washed, yo-ho-ho,
Easily overboard, merrily bobbing as water sloshed,
    yo-ho, o-
Ver the gunwhale, round the deck and back to its,
    yo-ho, h-
Eaving, sliding lair. At last it was still, but no-one cried
    Ahoy!;
Dead calm, empty, flat horizon. Days. *Swim for it.*

Did they know, now, what was coming, and did they
    fear it?
Rudderless; the paintwork blistered, cracked;
Outboard flooded: thus they found the boat, with seven
    crooked
Weals scratched in the fibreglass, no fishing gear,
No clothes, nothing, not a trace of Garth or Greer
Except for hanks of their hair – they had tied hooks to
    these,
Dangled them, watched fish take them and break them
    with ease.

MOTHS

That night I came home late and found
a moth flickering helplessly round and round
inside the lampshade. I went to help it.

The sixty-watt bulb had not shrivelled it
but its wings were scorched,
it was beyond help, almost beyond harm.

As it unwound slowly on my outstretched palm
it left a powdering of gold-dust
as fine as the blusher that streaked my T-shirt

where her cheekbone had brushed it,
its wing-beat was as powerful and as fragile
as the blink of an eyelash in the half-inch

of smoky air between us.
We'd sat as strangers lately introduced,
we'd chewed the fat and made a date for lunch

and my heart was fluttering when I asked her
to dance to an old one by Elvis.
It was tricky but she was lithe and agile

and had just fitted her pelvis
to mine when suddenly – someone had seen us,
she had to, she was sorry but, she was leaving.

Where's the harm? I wondered as, stood stewing
in my own body heat in a crowd of couples
melted together, I watched her bobbing and weaving

towards the powder-room. I left soon after.
In the taxi I thought, nothing doing,
this one's too hot to handle,

don't make that lunch, it's not worth the candle . . .
Next day I read, among other troubles,
that the place had been torched –

it seemed someone paid through the nose
for a deal that wasn't up to snuff, the upshot:
three women trapped in the Ladies choked to death

and were done to a turn. I caught my breath.
The moth had taken so long to die, God knows
that in the end I crushed it.

COBH

At East Ferry a boat's ribs curve out of blackened mud
like the blackened skeleton of a whale;
further down the coast road the docks are derelict,
the windows of sheds are smashed and on a weed-
   sprouting wall
someone has sprayed INTERNMENT KILLS; the broken
   derrick
and the rusting gantry loom prehistoric and mad
in the evening sky. You stand on one of the wharves
and look into the oily grey-brown waters of Cobh
and see a crab groping through a porthole like a cave
where brass is barnacle-encrusted and the sea-grass waves
to itself in the mirror that is turning back to sand
and a chandelier still gleams through the murk
when the camera catches it and shoals of fish shoot away
   from the sound
of the bathyscope as it bumps and scrapes along the
   Plimsoll mark.

THIRTY-FIVE

Window-box

You've come to this, your square of dark at rooftop level,
a square of light, a window-box – hers;
she busies herself in the kitchen while your grinning devil
slowly mists over. Everything blurs.

Hurrumph. You swipe a porthole clear.
Not funny any more: the patience of a saint
and her pottering have taken on
new purpose. Beddy-byes. You watch her disappear

through a wall, but you caught the scent
that time she loomed at the top of her bathroom stair,
a startle of white, a fuzz of hair . . .
Tonight, though, it's been hours and all she's done

is pour glass after glass of wine, hide her face
in her upturned hands as if resting her case
and sob. Anyway, her shoulders shake.
Earlier, you had a nasty shock –

she stood at the sink abstractedly washing a cup
and seemed to see you when she looked up:
peered as if the glowing point of your cigarette
was your eye, so fiercely

you'd been staring, and so long. The farce
that goes on night after night in secret –
your shyly peeping round the edge
of the window-frame, clutching the window-ledge.

Tea

A stranger thumbing through the obvious books,
the often-noticed tilt of her head
as she dangles a tea-bag in the vortex,
a phantom-imprint on the bed,
a perfume-trace, the ghost of one blonde hair;
between her tooth and lip, a thin saliva-thread,
her bra and slip, almost, slung on your chair . . .

The spoor of watch and earrings in the inch-thick dust.
The cream-or-lemon stain on the duvet. (You must
clean up this place, you must clean up your act.)

You've come to this, accessory after the fact.

MURPHY'S LAW

A step or two inside the door
this looks like all the other London boozers,
strawberry-nosed and ash-haired losers
and just what I'd been looking for:

red plush worn smooth and greasy, mottled,
carpet like a lunch of Jackson Pollock's,
nicotine-yellow ceiling, walls a light shit-brown shading
   to dark,
a choice of draught or bottled
and in the bogs, graffiti from the Ark –
Never mind the Sex Pistols, here's the bollocks . . .

The barmaid tilts a glass with practised hand
and in flows a black swirling sludge. She lets it stand
a minute, I stand transfixed. In flows some more.
You have to let it settle. Get what you settle for.

ECT

I had relinquished her that afternoon to the rule
of dial-switches,
skull-pads, rubber grips, ankle-straps,
spasms, twitches.

I had noted the soft bosom and hard eyes of an Irish sister
as my mother owned up in a whisper
to 'the occasional drink'.
I had noted the cabbagey,
piss-and-disinfectant stink.

Like a child abandoned to its first day at school
she looked at me in disbelief
as I receded, waving, from the ward.

She had left me once. I was three.
I was told only my mother 'wasn't very well'.
When she came back 'something had been murdered',
my father said. Her voice was quieter,
she often stood, clutching the sideboard,
swaying. She wouldn't let him near her.
Their only contact, week by week,
his morning-and-evening peck on one cheek.

*

(On a postcard that came from Madrid,
a recent vision, so it seemed, of Hell:
a high-walled, red-brick abattoir I recognized
    open-mouthed.
The look of disbelief, the shock
and terrible recoil, the buckled swaying . . .)

23

When I got back that evening from the hospital
your phone was off the hook,
as, I suppose, you believed you were.
When I started to shout and throw scraps
from your dustbin at the darkened windowpane
you were in the grip of something, I could hear,
your whole body shook
with strange convulsions . . . Not grief.
Not ECT. A newer therapeutic method.

Now you are spending the summer in Spain
and last night, ringed by faces, braying,
I watched him steady the twitching sword.

ART HISTORY
Fish-Market, Venice, by Sophie MacPherson

You remember your first great arrival in Venice –
at the fish-market, gold and silver scales
fell from your eyes

and into your pockets. A doubloon-hoard.
You remember your first shared, shuttered bed-and-board,
the dresser criss-crossed by a thousand little snails.

You remember the black curls
on Annie's mount of Venus,
the tracks of two snails strung like pearls.

Velvet

A room in Venice where our differences could be aired:
William Morris hangings, pearl-rich brocades,
a Fortuny dress brought out from under wraps
(she was Sybil Sassoon – in Orpen's portrait –
   to the life . . .)

So, our luck was in. Her small cry of relief
when I met her in rainy darkness at the station –
unmolested, she had crossed the barricades
carrying her huge valise, her superstition.

Years before, two soldier-boys had marched her
from a train to a hut in a railway-siding.
Between us lay the bayonet that had marked her.
'There's so much hate. I can't live in hiding . . .'

She shuddered at the Massacre of the Innocents.
We scared each other recalling *Don't Look Now*
and saw blood seeping out of every wall. 'No,
I can't go back . . . I have to . . . It's *insane.*'

When, a year later, she was 'running from all that'
on a tourist visa and her nerves, I met her at the airport –
she was an undesirable . . . And when she found Sophie's
Fish Market, Venice hanging in my poky flat,

with red flags – those great red drapes –
billowing on the colonnade, she stared, and stared . . .
Moving on, to Paris, Fontainebleau, 'somewhere . . . *apart*'
she left a crushed-velvet one-piece among my trophies.

STORM

At 2 a.m. she arrived out of the wild north wearing
her daffodil-yellow fisherman's coat – with warm
cheeks and a strange smell and swearing up a storm
at the minicab driver who'd tried to get a leg over
and ended by pulling a fast one. A half of Bells,
some fifteen B&H, and she was calm enough
to ferret through my albums with the white-denim furrow
of her tail in the air – at last we got off
on *Louise*, the girl *with perfect skin* and *cheekbones like
geometry* (at which point I brought in her own
perfect skin, and reached to stroke it), then someone else
who *looked like Eve Marie-Saint* and *read Simone
de Beauvoir* – as she does, or did; 'I'm not a dyke,
you know', she said suddenly as she burrowed
deeper into bed, and sleepy-drunk, I was all at sea . . .

CARAVAGGIO: SELF-PORTRAIT WITH SEVERED HEAD

I painted myself into a corner
of the *Martyrdom of St Matthew*
and it was as if I had proved the blade
on my own flesh and bone.
I half-hid in shadow
behind a pillar of a colonnade
and wished that I too might be turned to stone.

— As I almost was by Medusa's death-shriek,
or when, a few years after my *Matthew* triptych,
I grasped the smooth, muscly throat
of a boy who had lied
his way into my love and betrayed me,
and cut it. After the verdict of the coroner —
that my life and works posed 'a grave threat
to public morals' — I was hounded out of Rome
on a charge of homicide.

They might as well have cut off my painting arm.
Would they have put a price on my head
if they'd known how gladly I once drank
that same boy's blood,
and opened my own vein for him to drink?
If they had known how often
I had felt his thin cock stiffen
and jolt and slabber in my palm?

It hardly came as a surprise
when my 'friends in high places', bishops, cardinals even,
were afraid to stick their necks out as much as an inch –
I had repeatedly astonished their eyes
and tried to stir some compassion or pity
but would never have offered house-room
to either their piety
or their aesthetic sense:
in neither are they exactly given
to being moved, let alone to tears.

Is that little hustler for trade an icon?
Nothing could have saved him in the plague years –
not even those who feel themselves at one
with the helpless lookers-on
in my *Beheading of St John*.

MISSING

Messages. The dumb machine's small bright red eye
is blinking on and off, and I'm home and dry –
the cat uncurls and looks up, stretching, yawning
in a wedge of light between the windowsill and broken
    blind,
the grey-blue light of five-thirty in the morning . . .
The blue light was my blues, the red light was my mind . . .
Another half an hour and the adult video begins
once more behind my bloodshot, sleepless eyes:
is it life-saving, wrestling? Everybody wins, she pushes
    him away
but only to clutch him closer, surprise, surprise,
no dream-stewardess is offering me coffee, though it's day
coming red-eyed over the roofs, over the rim
of the world, bringing for me cat's-breath, for her: him.

*

Under-achieving, Underground-haunting, I descended to
a twilit flickering world, as I'd been led to expect;
I followed with my eyes the lighted windows rattling past
and found you out in one of them, moving too fast
for a sound to leave my open mouth. Could I detect
some sadness on your face, beautiful, downcast?
What assignation drew you on? There came a blast
of noise, a rush of foul air, a red light changed to green
somewhere far down the line, you did not look back,
and in your hurry to be moving you had not seen
how in another second you'd be changing track . . .
If you are Eurydice, could I be Orpheus, I mean
could anything I might still say or sing reclaim you?

*

Return, re-run, a dream of moon-reflecting sea,
a neon beach-bar, teenage crowd and glowing jukebox,
the screen alive with ghosts, the comical dubbed voices
and the couples sitting, knees drawn up on the sand;
we are drifting away from them, close and slow,
not talking, arms around each other's shoulders lightly –
the whole day's heat has soaked into our itching backs...
We kiss, your tongue is warm and quick, but something
   stops you,
you break away and run towards the sea, you turn and
suddenly, remembering *It's not like years ago*
the fear of getting caught   the recklessness in water
a flash of white your little gasp and you are swimming
   brightly
away from me   the undertow   *What if there were two*

*

Paris, and the boulevard I walked down with you
towards your mother's charming attic, your mother who
so charmingly stayed with friends while we played house
and fooled around; and here is the café where you sat
for me to take your picture, pouting *à la parisienne*;
here is the little bridge that crosses to the Ile St Louis
where you clutched me – though we were already late
for our rendezvous, for the movie, everything –
and opened your lips and said 'Kiss me! On ze mouse!';
here are the old men by their bookstalls, regarding me
   strangely
for here I am weeping, remembering *St Louis. Louis,*
   the Seine
cold-grey below, staring until one of them takes my arm
gently, and leads me nowhere, away from here, from harm.

*

Heroine of your teen romance, and so much a child
that when I called and found you swaddled on a sofa
in a kind of nappy (the 'thing' had split, you'd been
    emptied out
and the blood and after-pain were all you had to suffer)
you could smile at me, a dazed and happy smile
as I fed you cakes and poured champagne – sweet
    things . . .
We were celebrating, I was yours – why should you
    doubt? –
and had been since the night you shyly asked to stay,
unpeeled, unhooked, turned unhesitatingly
towards me, 'trembling with excitement' as you later said;
no thought for the thing flushed down, away,
no thought for the world that wasn't you and me,
no thought, now, for me (sweet things he told you 'turned
    your head').

*

You were quiet, in your bath, and you were going to sleep
    with him.
I knew it, the cat knew it. The bath-water felt it,
and the sliver of soap with which you soaped your quim,
the sponge with which you soaked your breasts, both
    smelt it –
when you clasped your nose and swiftly ducked
(sink or swim, you witch!) your hair waved like sea-grass,
your thatch, laid flat like tangled seaweed, foam-flecked,
lifted on the swell, and a slither of eel-slick skin
showed like the pearl-pink inside of a shell . . .
You surfaced, shifted slightly, settled your arse.
I saw it clenching tightly as his fingers gripped,
I saw your sea-anemone open, close as he plunged in.
Looking up, you smiled. I would say you slipped.

*

She moves on. She moves on,
taking with her when she's gone
your jacket, jeans and shirts,
your better self. It hurts and hurts.

She moves on. 'What this place needs',
she said when she first stayed the night,
'is a woman's touch.'
And she gave it that all right –
books trashed, clogged hairs in the sink;
she scarred your back, kneed you in the crotch,
told you that you stank of drink,
stabbed you in the heart. It bleeds and bleeds.

She moves on. Into another world,
one in which you don't belong
and one in which she never furled
her legs round yours, and the song
has changed, for ever, and is wrong:
not 'Marry me' or 'Let's do it'
but 'I want us to be friends.'
And you can see right through it,
and it claws and claws, and never ends.

She moves on. Now what she thinks
is that you didn't love her, not enough,
and that he's 'easy-going'. And it's tough,
your wanting her. It stinks.

She moves on. She doesn't call,
she won't come back, she's too far in,
her love was as fake as her leopardskin,
as quickly shed. You fall and fall.

She moves on. Like a single cell,
like a virus, with as much in mind,
as much concern for what it leaves behind,
as much speed. And it's hell, it's hell.

Missing, believed lost, five feet four-and-a-half
of warm girl, of freckled skin and sulky laugh
and blood on the sheets and ash on the pillow
with the smell of bacon eggs and lubricant – how that
    lingers –
for breakfast; crumpled things to scoop up from the floor
and press against my face, and cunt-smell on my fingers;
I'll skip the part about love it seems so silly and low
– the aftertaste of afternoons in a strange bed in a
    stranger's
flat, 'I love the way you go down on me', breathless,
    'more.
Harder', and a red dress from the wardrobe, and the
    dangers:
at 3 a.m. your boot like a bad dream pounding on the
    door
and the way that anything you wanted could be true,
if you said it was. But not this. Missing. You.

                                    *

Over. It's over. Three words uttered matter-of-factly
that I hear over and over in the sound of the wheels
hissing through rain, pointed north, as I drift in and out of
    sleep
on the back seat, remembering our scenes, line by line,
    exactly
remembering line by line the words that tell you how it
    feels

to have brought this sadness with you from the womb
remembering *I could turn you inside out* on the car stereo
you swung like a handbag to our hotel room
and your body kneeling, bent double, face buried in the
    duvet,
remembering how I stayed awake all night to watch you
    sleep,
lips parted, eyelids flickering *She is so beautiful she is so
    young and Oh*
our drive next day through driving rain, our bickering
I can't stand this, give me 'Les douleurs', give me Dufay

*

Viera Lodge: a drystone wall and one bent tree
and nothing else between us and the boiling sea,
the slate-grey, roiling sea. The wind wails
and we are safe inside, drinking, hearing how
a boy from the island, nineteen, hanged himself for love
of a girl up for the holidays from Glasgow.
And suddenly, for no reason, or for love,
I see myself walking down the slight slope of lawn
in the awful slate-grey light of dawn,
the cat prowling round an empty flat, listening for the key
in the lock, racing after shadows; red sails
in the sunset, a profile in the prow – it's you –
a world away from where I lie, bloated, blue.

*

Every move you make, every step you take – the
  'disco-deck'
throbs, a blaze of glory as the evening flashes, fades;
waterlight flushes us, glass after glass brings back the blood
to day-defeated faces, each one doing its best
to hide a grey fatigue. You are not here, we flash and fade
as the loud, lit boat glides through London, I am
  obsessed –
in a small saloon, a scattering of couples watch the end
of *L'Atalante*, then *Ai No Corrida*, cries and whispers
  drowned
by the throbbing engine. You saw it with a girlfriend
and called to say, 'I need you, now. Can I come round?' –
I turned you away. My stomach churns, I turn and wade
  through dreck
of bodies – every vow you break, every smile you fake –
that twist and writhe in water, clutch and clasp in mud.

*

She came racing towards me, across a dancefloor
littered with tables, bottles, petals; she wore a flower
behind her ear, her hair piled high on her head,
wisps falling carelessly; my child-bride, my sweet
stamped her foot, one side then the other, flamenco-style,
gathered her skirt in both hands, by the hem,
and tugged it, left, right, in time with her stamping feet;
raced towards me, zig-zagged, in front of me, behind,
a challenge in her eyes and in her wide white smile . . .
It's crazy what you could have had, it's crazy what you
  could have had,
it seems a shame to waste your time to me – R.E.M.
remind me, I re-wind, replay, I know by heart
that was just a dream Pause Stop *I need this* Start

*

Now that I no longer sleep,
now I could no more count sheep
than the nights they spend together, or apart,
now I pray she'll have a heart
and come back, and come back,
now I stare into a black
and featureless night that goes on
and on, a grey and featureless dawn,
now that the telephone is quiet
and the memory runs riot,
now that I mix up the days
and am fuck-all use in several ways,
now that she's safely in the sack
with someone else, and won't come back,
now that I'm rotted through and stink
of loneliness, self-pity, drink,
now that she's finally taken off
and I'm left here to shake and cough
and wait for my first heart-attack
or for her to wake up and come back,
now that no-one wants to know
who I see, what I do or where I go,
now that more flee from me each week,
the women who sometime did me seek,
than I've had dinners on my plate,
now that her love has turned to hate
I think of this: the open-handed way I had
of slapping her, her lovely face, her head,
and making her see stars,
or pushing her downstairs
and out of the door. There's more —

Open me, the book says – *Cherokee*, by Jean Echenoz –
when I brush it, hunting up something else, and so I do,
and on the title-page, an entry-wound, black and yellow-
brown,
the words 'Hole by Murphy, summer 1991' –
the ash dropped from your cigarette, your head dropped in
a doze
to your chest, and the paper burned right through
to page thirteen; the sun in Brittany burned down,
your head jerked upright from its dream, your face was
flushed
and freckled, your plump pale arms and shoulders turning
red –
had your mother seen, your aunt seen? They went on
sipping tea
and talking. Was it that day you wrote 'Nom d'une pipe,
tu me manques' and sent the postcard that flutters now
from the book
you gave back sheepishly, unread? (Tearstains by Alan,
1993.)

*

Night, the roof is leaking, and I perform my dance
with saucepan and bucket, and the steady drip, drip
of dirty water tells how love leaked out of my life;
for two years, I tried to stop the holes and fill the cracks
but there were always more, and the slow drip of slights,
insults, screaming on the telephone, hanks of hair
yanked out, left a stain that spread everywhere.
So now that the roof leaks, and the cat looks askance
at my attempts to catch as I would a second chance
these drops like huge tears falling from black heights,
I drink up regret, to the last drop,
and stop and let it all come down in cataracts
to drown me: night and rain and the thought of my
not-wife.

JELLYFISH

Did she fall, or was she pushed?
The talk was more than usually hushed –
Mary Decker, Zola Budd –
when we got back from three days in Donegal.

You'd hired the car 'to take a skite around' –
turfstacks, marram, the scrotumtightening sea.
As we ducked the imaginary badminton net
rigged up in your back entry,
Mary was in the pantry;
she turned from the sink, half-peeled spud
in one hand, palette knife in the other. 'Paul,
that priest's here again. He wants to know
do we live as man and wife.' Your face was white.
I went upstairs – her 'Blue Speckled Torso'
hung above the bed – until she called my name.

A glass of chilled wine. We sat and ate:
a salmon, drawn by the magnet of itself
from west to east – or was it
the other way about? – to end,
the raw and the cooked, on everyone's plate.
Not much was said. 'Would you and your friend
like some more?' I'd never known anyone
so self-possessed, so at home
with the knowledge that nothing could last –
not her work, or yours, not Landseer Street, not Belfast . . .

You had just explained that you could rhyme
silicon and *silicone*, since both are found
in *a pebble of quartz* – etymologically –
when Warren Zevon sang out from the stereo,
If Cali-forn-ia slides in-to the Ocean,
like the mystics and statistics say it will . . .
and I saw, in slow motion,

the West Coast sheer off and slip underwater, and,
a million or so years after that, some
gentle creature slope out of soupy slime
where we'd parked the car and walked the strand,
scrutinize a shoal of un-biodegradable
silicone implants flopped on the sand,
then turn away, no more apt to guess how far they'd come
from their origins, or the stir
they'd once caused in the human breast, than we
to scry our future, let alone Mary's fate
in a score of beached jellyfish that stared
up at us, and stared, and stared, and stared.

THE QUILT

for Paul Muldoon

We were walking home from Pig Heaven
(that, to everyone else, was warmed-over hell)
and there it was, in a thrift-shop window
not three blocks from where
a whole cinema had stamped its feet and cheered
with fear and pity, fear and guilt
when Glenn Close slid back blood-smeared
in her final bath: a pretty patchwork quilt.

It was gorgeous, all-American and old,
at least a hundred years old. It was New York City
and the Prairies seen from the air.
I thought of Jean, and wanted it for her.
I couldn't stretch to it. I hadn't even
brought a wedding-present – unless you counted
the watercolour of a chipped Chinese bowl
that hung now, framed and mounted,
in your kitchen (you had given me the bowl . . .)

Five years on, I think of Quilty, Clare,
pursued by Humbert to his funny-farm
and, dying, gathering the blankets round himself,
and of the quilt that keeps warm, keeps from harm
each all-American boy newly come to grief.
Take this quilt, take it home to Hopewell
and lay it gently on a sleeping Dorothy Aoife.

CASE-HISTORY

She were the last one we ducked
in Morning Pond. She were doggy-fucked
by the Fiend in the shape of a white alsatian.
That dog went on to devour
two little girls on Morning Common.
She were an evil woman.
We done it in one session.
It took about two hour.

                    *

She was a witch,
some said. Lived alone,
her habits grown
round her shambles
of a house
like brambles
and lichen-covered stone;
her familiars
a flea-bitten cat,
a blind rat, a mouse –
all four sleeping
in moth-eaten furs ...
Peculiar bitch.
   At thirty-five,
no-one's wife
or daughter,
no-one's friend,
she watched TV,
watched seasons creeping
towards their end,
heard starlings bicker
on the roof-tree;
knitted baby-things
by the flame-flicker
of a single candle,
and frigged herself

with the handle
of an old kitchen-knife,
shouting her name
and the prayer
daddy taught her
when she came.
   But she had nights
when, standing out there
in the lane, in the dark,
she fancied she saw,
caught in the stark
moon-glow, or wavering
in the headlights,
a hobgoblin face,
her father's face –
she could hear
the swish of cars,
sometimes a screech,
a muffled shout,
a little thump
and recoil as each
small shadow life
was put out,
eyes like dead stars;
could hear once more
her own blood-smear
splosh into the sump.

                    *

At dawn, she blinked at dew-glitter on a frosted pelt –
squirrels, hedgehogs, foxes. She watched a thick ooze seep,
a spreading oil-slick, a warm slow pitch
puddling in the ruts of roadside, ditch.

When she turned over, moaning, in her sleep
what was it she muttered? What was it she felt
when she ran out in her flowered nightgown
and waited for a car to knock her down?

What could the drivers see,
as they jerked awake with time to spit
their *Fucking Christ!*, behind the apparition (*Shit!*)
each swerved round as if it were a tree?

And when they freed from leaf-burial, bracken-snare
her father's rotted flesh and bones (flesh
of her flesh), did she feel her hard face flush,
and turn away from sickening air?

                              *

When my healing hand moves to touch
her cropped head, the pelt stiffens, rises;
shrinking in a corner of her hutch
she cracks the shrivelled, thin disguises,
the words I throw her, and scents hostile breath,
bitter as the kernel, as some foul broth.

BEASTS

The corner video club has got in *Babes of Satan*
and Sandra's made black candles. Frank from Tidy Tots
has promised to run up some cloaks in shiny satin
since Babs' and mine got spoiled last time – blood got on
   my tits
with spunk and other stuff that won't wash off. It was
   great
when Mr Lumley from the chemists used the cross
on Sandra and she squealed so much you really had to grit
your teeth until it sort of poured out – like the curse
only, you know, you could see a bit more what it was.
Sandra fainted, so she missed the part with the oven.
Keith and Babs and me did it all different ways
while Mr Lumley said the words. I've got to help the coven
by getting knocked up too, Keith says. It's more fun than
   'Sting's'
on a Friday night. Keith's seen a picture of Frank's niece –
eight or nine, looks great in hot pants and a halter
top. We're round at Frank's this time. She's called Denise.
I seed they give me sumthing and I was sreched on a allter.
I sore reel men in hoods. There big red things.

45

PERSONAL

Tonight we have a game called Bits and Pieces,
in which she hands me some of his old loves
saying she wants me to have them. Silk scarves,
handkerchiefs. A silver hip-flask. Halves
of plump fob-watches, stopped in 1910.
The slender cigarette-case, too slender for
my flavourless, filtered smokes. I smooth the creases
in a pair of dainty chamois leather gloves.

Some of them *his* mother handed on.
The rest are Shepherd's Bush and Chelsea Arts, pre-war
Bohemian and dandyish. Except his dog-tag,
indestructible, 1119681;
and this ring I always thought his wedding-ring
but which he wore, she says, 'for luck. A personal thing.'

SWANS

Moonlight on the river Drim – the *Black* Drim,
that is – and we two on the concrete promenade, and
  a black
swan all the way from Avon. *Why* (as I stroked your
  back),
this is Illyria, lady (This is not a dream).

             *

When, our last night at the Hotel Drim
you pushed me unprotesting out of your room
because I stank of beer and would not stop
singing, out of tune, *I'll take you to the top*
you looked at me with the exact same air –
of mild astonishment that might, any moment, flare
into pure disdain – as the unruffled swan
that registered its disapproval and passed on
with a flurry of wing-feathers, a frown
when the tall birch creaked like a mast in mid-ocean,
creaked and – gracefully, in slow-motion,
with its rigging of twigs and branches, splitting the glade
where, at long trestle-tables in the shade
four-dozen singing birds, drinkers and eaters
were toasting each other in imperfect metres,
silencing the gypsy band, the amplified croon
of local party-girls through the heat-struck afternoon –
leaned towards the lake and crashed down.

PORTRAIT OF A LADY

She's been in too deep and out too far, oh *man*,
her dark eyes spill nearly twenty years of bruises,
roll-ups and cider, and a battered Morris van
holds everything she ever wants or uses –
her Dylan tapes, her Steeleye Span and Fleetwood Mac
(he told her once she looked like Stevie Nicks,
and 'Go Your Own Way' still takes her back),
her daughter's scribbles, her I-Ching spill-sticks,
the bag of grass hand-picked from her veggie patch,
some tattered old Viragos, Mervyn Peakes
and a book of newish poetry. There's a catch
in her voice as she half-sings, half-speaks
the slow blues she wrote about him when he left,
that neither of you will remember by the morning
when you have to leave as well and she offers you a lift
through dripping lanes – but it draws you, yawning,
shivering, to huddle in the pile of blankets, quilts
while she clings close, and seems on the edge
of tears; your breath, the frost-blurred ghosts and guilts . . .
We're gonna meet, she tells you, *meet on the ledge*.

HOUSEBOY

I remember the day you brought him home
slung on the back seat of the Renault,
minus one of his slender papier-mâché arms.
Sad-eyed, big-eyed jungle boy,
his skin a delicate café-au-lait,
he stood in Greenwich among the scented leaves
of macramé-gardens, bedroom tendrils, ferns.
The baby in the bulrushes and a god by turns
he watched over both our lives.
One night I caught you staring, arms akimbo,
at the gentle, sexless slope of his groin:
'I can't help feeling that he feels a lack . . .'
Next moment you were back
with an itsy-bitsy leopardskin G-string.

These days, the stylized pastel palms
on my bathroom walls, the split bamboo
that frames the shaving-mirror, are all he knows
of home, and it seems to me he has grown
more melancholy in my service –
he is custodian of the lavatory bowl,
spirit of the little waterfall. He holds
the stringless, 'unseasoned and unsupple' bow
a friend left when he went west for good and all.
You ferried me, the boy, but not yourself,
with my suitcases and a box
of played-out albums and unread books,
to de Beauvoir Road, where he came to grief –
he lost a leg, another arm – then Ladbroke Grove.

Where you and I later came to grief.
I broke us up, that is, without a second thought
and all he could do was look on
as you ran weeping to the bathroom
(his biggest yet) to spit me out.
Way above his head here, on a shelf
the Tampax, baby-oil and cotton-wool
are no longer yours, or anyone's.
His only other distraction
two volumes of satanic verses.
Which leaves him free to wistfully recall
my getting back that early afternoon
to find you in, our urgency, our flushed replies –
the footsteps, the shouting from the hall;

or watch me plunge and root for cufflinks
and come up with two solder-drops, black shiny tears
on two curls of gold-plated wire
that slipped, once, through your earlobes –
your worthless, second-favourite pair
of earrings (when did you leave them?);
watch me take in for the nth time
the white, almost-transparent
skin of your neck; tears and mascara, Indian inks
that streaked your face; tiny tears
in the black curls round your other lips . . .
Does he imagine you as you were,
a towel-turban falling to your shoulder
when you stepped from the shower in a Luton hotel

where I fumed and fretted, waiting for take-off
to a tropic isle, a coconut grove, a forest?
(We'd won the trip, but on a technicality –
it was vaguely disgraceful, I hadn't come first.)
In that room with mini-bar, trouser-press, tea-things
you eased my fear of flying, that is of dying . . .
We never thought I'd grow this much older,
and the boy sees me shake off
sleep each morning with increasing disbelief; his blueish,
greenish, fluorescent hair's as thick as ever;
his vine-leaf garland keeps its rosy blush.
A sad inscrutable smile still plays,
etc. For his sake, come back. It's not over.
Come back to the ashram. Wield a new broom.

BAUDELAIRE

Two lovers, and that word, *infected*.
The red and black, black and red
of Hubert's boxes, a hundred pills in each.
The bravery in every word that's said,

in the small-talk and the tall tales of Sylvia Beach
and the offhand epitaph for Christopher Cox,
'He's dead, of course, like everybody else.'
The lucky life I've led.

The lucky life I've led
here, for three whole days,
not having thought once in all that time
of my rivals, of my wasted prime,

of her penchant for surprising herself,
her reaching for the bookshelf
above the bed
in the poky little box

above the rue de Rivoli – the smells
of smoke and sweat and semen, trapped air,
trapped lives – and reciting Baudelaire,
of his black and red

striped wallpaper and his darkened windows,
the black and red that filled his eyes
when it came to him that everybody dies
and that he would soon be dead,

her freckled shoulders shouting *Health*,
the toxic tears I shed,
my taking her by force and by stealth,
the venom I injected.

WEST 11TH STREET

for Bruno Fonseca

Night after starry New York night, I swung away from
    laughter
outside the White Horse, steered an uncertain course
to West 11th Street, dropped on all fours
and crawled up the creaking stairs to the great height
of the attic play-pen, where I scribbled till first light.

I was missing Anna then, and night after
starry night, I conjured her from E. J. Bellocq's
Storyville Portraits, palming myself off
over one particular photograph.
And once, sweating bourbon, I emptied my bollocks

on the blanket, tonguing Sally S——'s cleft –
she'd rescued me from outside an East Village bar
where, lifted off my feet and just as suddenly unhanded,
I'd flown a little way, and landed
face-down on the rain-soaked sidewalk, cheek pressed
    to a star.

The attic's a nursery now, and not a trace is left
of all that carry-on and lah-di-dah, not a whiff
of beer-breath, Camel-stench, not a snort or sniff
of bad cocaine, not a glimpse of a single starry night
anywhere in its innocent blue-and-white . . .

Back after six years, I sat round the kitchen table
with Richard and Elizabeth, and the talk avoided death
but I recalled how, the night before, you'd come in,
how the coat hung off your bones, how shockingly thin
your hair and beard were, and how each breath

rattled in your chest – you were 'stable'
but everyone, yourself included, knew that soon, soon,
your beautiful El Greco face would be gone, your mother
mourning her son, and Isabel, Caio, Quina their brother;
the light in your eyes already looked as pale as the moon

in your lovely 'Casa i lluna',
your speech was slurred by drugs, and too slow
for us to take up our ten-year conversation about
    Caravaggio;
and sometimes, though trying to be there, you were
    elsewhere,
on your daily pilgrimage to the Met, in the blinding air

of the Zattere, painting through the starry nights of
    Barcelona
or thinner and thinner on your final bed . . .
And none of this, not Dick's best friend being dead,
not the thought that you would soon be dead,
not the paintings that would stay forever in your head,

made any sense; no more did it make sense
that my last words to you should be a lame 'Take care',
that I should see, as I said them to the telephone, your
    thinning beard and hair,
that I should climb through the starry night above Newark
towards a loved face, and all that uphill work,

that I should wake from a dream of innocence
to sunrise in the window and sun-dazzle on the wing
of the 747, a white floor below, and empty heaven the
    exact same blue
as the blue on the nursery wall; that Dylan should sing
'Tangled up in Blue' on the in-flight stereo, that *On
    Being Blue*

should be open on my lap with a postcard of Miró's
'Blue II' to mark my place; that after six years
your great light should be going out
with you not even half-way done, that I should doubt
and again doubt my little light and dissolve in tears

in taxis, on autumn streets, in front of mirrors;
that upstairs in the attic, a new life should have gotten
    started,
that I should sit and listen to its soft breath on the
    intercom
with Dick and Betty, broken-hearted,
pouring wine and making plans; that I should find a home,

after six years, there on West 11th Street
in the very house that you and Isabel both had to leave
for Barcelona, London, so that you could live
and work and breathe, that I should leave it for the blue
    and white
of my flat and sit and try to fly a kite

of words like the boy you sketched for me, try to keep it
    straight
as the outflung arm of the David you sketched to make a
    point,
the sling still in his hand; that you should not paint
and paint, your strength still with you, and your sight,
your arm outflung to the starry night.

BATHTIMES

*'Meeting of the waters': curious natural phenomenon
caused by the meeting of different coloured waters of two
rivers which run side by side without getting mixed.*
(Tourist brochure, Manaus)

I meant to push the boat out, Murphy,
some time around the start,
not of our voyage but its third year –
to hoist full sail on our little brig
and make for the open sea,
to quit my quarters
in the stern, in the stew,
and stop behaving like an Admiralty prig;
throw overboard the spoilt governess,
the pressed man, raving, the mutinous crew;
take the helm and steer us
by all the stars
to a place of fewer storms than calms . . .

But you threw out bathwater-baby-Captain Bligh
and left me to sink or swim,
paddling my pirogue
at 'the meeting of the waters' –
one black, one rust-brown; left me high and dry
to frig and frot myself, toss and turn
and fret and fume
and watch a watermark, a stain
descend the bathroom wall
like the coastline of Brazil
on an old chart dotted with palms,
watch the pebbles, shells, dried seaweed
slip under grimy dust and disappear.

Have I gone to seed? Have I, my arse . . .
It's just that, adrift
with my harpoon gun
and native charms
I could go a week or more
without hearing word from anyone –
only the groan and creak
of timbers, the protesting shriek
of gulls, and, when I might think
I was set to go ashore
to surf and flowers and yells, the sift
of black and rust-brown sands in an hourglass
that looks like a twisted heart.

SOMEONE'S LIFE

In a sentence or two
from someone's Life
of someone else
who has become you,
you carry plastic bags
with yoghurt, cutlets, peas,
bread, ham and cheese
to your mother's house
which was once your house,
past windows in backs
of houses that were never yours,
windows, walls, doors
which open on lives
that were never yours;
lives no-one tells
(there is no-one to tell),
lives one could not hope,
in chapter after chapter,
in a single life, to capture:
in which, any moment,
someone will lift
an oval of Pears soap
from the scallop-shell
where it slithers in its glop
as, once, the scallop,
and feel in his palm
the child's glass oval
he would agitate
to watch a blizzard drift
and swirl and settle
round manger, shepherds, kings –
then holding out his arm
and tilting it slowly
he sees them, glowing
in that richly tinted globe,
caught in the amber

of a suburban twilight,
of a late-Edwardian summer
that like the Empire
went on and on for ever
through Sundays without number
of fish-paste and cucumber:
grandfather and grandmother
pouring tea like a river
in Africa or India
as hot sun pouring
through the bathroom skylight
glints on the tea-things
and George V, Queen Mary
and a cluster of aunts and uncles
look on sternly, glaring
from their ovals
of burnished metal . . .
He will take scissors, talc
from a crowded shelf,
dry and dress himself
and go downstairs
to the sound of talk
from a sitting-room
at the door of which
he stops and stares:
at row on row
of burnished frames
propped on the piano,
at women's floppy hats
and shapeless dresses,
girls' amazing tresses,
flannel bags and spats;
the talk has stopped,
nobody is there
and he does not know
whose life this is from —
this dust-filled air,

these faint smells
of lavender and cat's-piss,
these sofas, chairs,
these wedding-pictures,
watercolours, this
grandfather-clock,
its one hand stopped,
this rabbit-gun
with the broken stock;
someone's, not yours,
not his, but theirs,
all this, nobody's Life
that no-one tells –
husband and wife
for forty years,
the husband dead and gone,
the wife living on
with cats for company;
shuffling, she appears
in the kitchen door
and you set down
plastic bags, take out
from your bountiful store
bread, ham and cheese,
yoghurt, cutlets, peas
and say, to this
helpless, frightened woman
who was once your life,
whose life now is you,
'Mother, sit down.
Here is your cup of tea,
there the supper I will make
in a sentence or two.'

AUBADE

Birdcall loud at five;
the slap of rain
against the grey window-pane,
the slow drip of being alive.

A goods train judders
to an anguished halt,
the pipes digest their fault,
the cat yawns and shudders.

And quickening fear
beats in my chest –
I reach for your shoulder, breast
but you are not here.